Seasons of the Heart Garden of the Soul

A Poetic Journal

Elsie Wood

ISBN: 978-1-6847-1543-5 (sc)
ISBN: 978-1-6847-1544-2 (e)

Lulu Publishing Services rev. date: 01/16/2020

Dedicated to
family, friends
mentors - present and past
who gave me wings to fly.

With deepest gratitude to my life partner, soul mate
who supports and encourages my dreams.

Contents

Summer

Autumn

Endings

Beginnings

Starting My Journey

The twists and turns a life will take are hard to imagine. I can best describe my life as a journey of discovery. Early on I learned that change was a given and I had choices to make how I would embrace those changes. Sometimes I felt I was in control and other times I was flailing, floating, drowning in a stormy sea of change.

Many times I experienced synchronous and serendipitous events in my life which set a direction altering my path..

And so it is that I find myself now past my three-quarters of a century milestone, aiming to continue my wanderings, wonderings and living out my dreams hopefully past my century milestone. Mary Oliver's line from her poem, *The Summer Day*, " Tell me, what is it you plan to do with your one wild and precious life? " has been my touchstone in helping me to navigate the twists and turns. Ten years ago I was in a women's circle, a group of like-minded souls all seekers, searchers and creatives, facilitated by a gifted, highly skilled painter, Sunny Brown, who graciously shared reflections on life, art and wisdom.

I started a journal then whose cover I titled *Seasons of the Heart, Garden of the Soul,* never imagining that I was planting seeds for what has transpired this year.

I serendipitously stumbled across my old journal and the title was the inspiration for the theme for a CreativeSage-ing Circle I facilitate. At the same time I joined a Poetry, Lyrics and Words writing group and began writing poems to mark my journey through the seasons; tending and caring for the garden of my soul.

I thank you, Dear Reader, for coming along on my journey.

Starting My Day
An Invocation

I bless this day with the rising of the sun
Today I stand in wonder
     I walk in wisdom
     I am in spirit
     I am open to possibilities
Today is the beginning of the *rest* of my life
Today is the beginning of the *best* of my life
I am grateful for this new day.
Thank you for the *Present*.
Blessings upon all - great and small.
May it be so

I am mindful to begin my day with this Invocation.
It sets the tone of the day, with gratitude, presence, intention and openness.
I make time to get centered, read, write, journal in prose or poetic form, and enjoy a bit of day-dreaming.

Winter

Happy New Year!

A new year is
almost here.
Where has the old year gone,
It's time for moving on.

So many things left to finish.
Do I let go or grimace.
Do I move them to the new year.
But my time is so dear.

Priority is but an illusion
as it shifts minute by minute.
Pay close attention
Mindful of the reason and season.

Happy New Year!

A new start is here,
To yourself be kind.
And treasures you will find
Let magic fill your mind.

Make each moment count
What's next will come in time
Stay open for possibility,
Embrace life and creativity.

Happy New Year!

Greeting the New Year

It's late it's late
   It just can't wait
      The past is gone, so
         Time for moving on
            Wheels are turning
            Cycles spinning
               From year to year
               Time is passing.
                  Seasons come, seasons go
                  Colors changing
                  Time for engaging
                     Every month of every year
                     Every day of every month
                     Every hour of every day
                       Every minute of every hour
                         Every second of every minute...
                         Be!

Winter

Wisdom won from winter's glory

I am embraced; a fluffy white blanket surrounds me.

Napping: to energize the gloomy day

Time for ruminating, remembering and reflecting

Embodied sensations

Roots resting, waiting for the wakening

March Begins

Dust motes dancing in the air
   in silent song without a care.

Dawn has come and gone
   and March begins softly,
      like a gently gliding swan.

I ponder as to what this day will bring
   a precious gift not to be ignored
   to fill with mindful action is my wondering
      adding meaning, mystery to my life adored.

Winter Dreams

Where do winter dreams go
   To a fantasy land with unreachable stars?
   To a thick darkened forest where shadows lie?
   To a childhood home where family secrets hide?
   To a comforting nest where memories sleep?
   To a wonderland with nature's delight -
     with glistening snow and sun so bright.
To a silence profound with no one around
     to dwell and soar to heights unbound.
To a window-filled room dispelling the gloom
To a comfy cozy chair and a book.
To bask in the Present in my sacred nook

The Present - Ode to Rising Sun

Brilliant fire-y orb
Vista of wonder and awe.
Yummy Dreamsicle.

Winds of Change

Morning reverie accompanied by
  the wind's shushing and sighing
Mother Nature flexing her muscles again
  the strong, sturdy pines succumb to bending and swaying

My thoughts flit caught by the wind,
  carried by clouds appearing beyond,
Meek and mild, mysterious and mighty
  soothes, cools, upends and razes.

Life goes on with wind- wrought changes
  the urging reminder of moments so fleeting
My choices made by the blowing tune shout
  be true to your soul, that's what life is about.

A Spin of a Coin

Wander down the path with me
   I'll share what I see; please share what you see
For a coin with same faces just doesn't exist
   It's with two unique sides made, not to resist
but to travel together, discover the world
   two sides of a story is what needs to be told

Each view is two-sided, each moment it's changed
   With perception and perspective it gets rearranged
At times its upended and sideways and skewed
   With two sets of eyes, it's hard to be misconstrued
Like the bare branched tree is ugly you say
   And full of potential, I say, as it waits the warm day.
Your choice is to interpret the spin of the coin
   My hope is for shared understanding and vision to join.

Walk About

It's good for the heart, so I've been told
Your body will love it as you get old.
A hike in the woods is yet even better
It engages the senses regardless of weather
A high mountain road with breath-taking views can't be beat
Of value as well, feet pounding on side-walked urban street
A treadmill session at home or a gym fills the bill
Get the heart pumping, avoid feeling over the hill.

Great medicine for the body but what's good for the soul?
What does it take for us to feel whole?
Asking right questions is a good start.
Vitamins for the spirit as well as the heart.
First one's, a bitter pill to swallow
Who am I? No time or place to wallow.
True to one self, all life's pieces fall into place
For a mind's walk about fills our heart with grace.

Awakening to Spring

It can be overwhelming not knowing the way,
but it is what you do along the way that matters.
                                        by Madisyn Taylor

Awaken sleepy Muse for the days grow longer
   for soon you'll hear the rumblings and feel the pangs of hunger.

Dormant winter dreams of wondering and wandering
   nourished by imagination's fertile ground
   begin the clamoring and stretching
   seeking expression to be found.

Purpose and direction - that's my stumbling block
Striving to answer Mary Oliver as what to do with my life.

It's not the What that stumps me as ideas come round the clock.
It's knowing and truth to Divine Calling that often brings me strife.
It's finding compassion and balance in the being and the doing.
It's ever mindful of the moment to gratefully usher in the Spring.

Dreamtime

Do birds rehearse their song in dreams?
Do bears dream of salmon-fishing in the stream?
A magic carpet ride to places unknown.
Seeds of creative imagination are sown.

Simple Pleasures

It's the beat of your heart that starts me dancing.
It's the clown in your eyes that keeps me laughing.
It's the joy in your day that leaves me smiling.
It's the love you have for me that fills my living.

A Perfect Day

What does a perfect day look like
   when there are more days past than tomorrows?

That crossed my mind, greeting the new day -
   Moon beans streaming - brightening the room.
A sensed treat offered.
   The moon, an eroding crescent edge is waning perfection,
its brightness in cloudless sky - a gift made -
      moon shadows dancing,
exaggerated piney silhouettes lay splayed
      upon earth's white velvet blanket -
a breath caught in wonder -
      the miracle of a small step on brilliant surface.

And so my day begins.

New day, new dawn
      The Present
         A breath of morning air -
Night's winter storm chased by
         eye-dazzling sunrise morn.
Awe-filled. How does it get better than this?

Nature provides, we abide. Body rhythms,
   Awakening circadian clock: sluggish or engaged;
   routines followed, patterned behavior.
A - biding time of mindful moments.
Stop - Breathe. Take a moment - breath inhaled with wonder
The moment savored with exhale extended.

Spring

Ode to Spring

Full moon, Super moon
  Spring Equinox brings the light.
Dispel winter blues.

Paint the Moon

Dark clouds blanket the sun's rising
There's a dampness in the air
I greet the day with a chill in my bones
Lone bird trills a morning song in woeful tones.

The gloom and doom is of our creation
Search for beauty and truth - the truth to set us free
    found in the ground, the sky, a breath, meditation
The art of the moment, the moment of art is transformation.

In my mind's eye I paint the waning super moon
    it's memory dispels the gloomy start
I fill my soul with joie de vivre and happy thoughts
        And ponder my gifts with a grateful heart.

Belonging

The place of my belonging
  Soothes my soul of longing.
Bliss is beauty; beauty bliss

Choices

Like so many flavors in an ice cream store
   choose one, perhaps two but you really want more.
A little of this, a little of that; narrowing wants
   standing here to decide, another comes to the front.
A flavor is chosen without hesitation or doubt
What would it be like to bring that about?

Life choices: some easy, some hard
   some are tried quickly, others hard to discard.
The latter's the challenge as often others involved
   whose feelings would hurt so I have discovered.
Words and actions affect us: right/wrong is in question
Golden silence is weighed against confrontation.

Platitudes, attitudes - many times guide the way
   give benefit of doubt, take least resistant path,
   don't let sun go down on anger.
Bury the pain, smile at the hurt, pretend it's okay.
   What is the final cost of not getting your way?
Some walk to the left, some to the right,
some meander, or go astray.
   When paths cross, meet with intention, attention and grace
Be true to oneself with a grin on your face.
   And with compassionate heart just simply sway.

Random thoughts

Yesterday
An article on Mary Oliver
A celebration of her life
A mindfulness poet
Poetry of awe
Hurt, pain, angst, sorrow
Seen through Nature's healing lens

Today
News on radio today
Nature, please show me the Healing Way
National leaders, predominantly male
  with rhetoric in question
  a country's well-being tended without much reflection
For well-intentioned actions, ending in mis-direction
  need conscious soul-searching drive for perfection.
Lies, fraud, collusion
  is it all an illusion?
Merely more delusion?
A wall to build, to protect
  or simply a ploy to reject.
To turn a blind eye to those in need, I object.

Tomorrow

National crisis, personal crisis, it's such a mess
How to move forward is difficult, I confess
To begin the healing takes one small step.
To do no wrong, to love - all religions agree
Begin now to be mindful and smile
a helping hand makes life worthwhile.

Sitting in Wonder

The gift of a new day
   Like magic: dark to light
The ancients marked its entry
   with reverence and delight.
The Present given to me.

Begin the day with exuberance
   not knowing what the day will bring
Choices to make; leave the doing to chance
   be creative and laugh - that's the only thing.
The start of a wonder-full dance

Breaking the Silence

Silence rules as the day breaks
   the blanket of quiet pulled off as Nature wakes.
Invited to listen, I stretch and sheets rustle
   my breath heard as I ready to hustle and bustle.

The sun barely seen upon the horizon.
   It's Spring! One bird sings, another echoes way over yon.
The dull hum of traffic from the canyon below
   breaks this sweet concert and soon I must go.

A moment of reflection sets the tone of the day.
The Present received with a smile on my face.
Long list of To Do, options and priorities to weigh.
My heart says, "Just play!" in this wonder-full place.

All in a Day

There aren't enough minutes in a day
   to do all I want to do.
So I pick a little here and
   and I wander over there.
The morning starts with
   a grateful practice and a prayer.
Breakfast soon follows with my love
   and crossword puzzle to solve.

And now the fun begins
   with no demands on me to be anywhere
   I choose to fill the hours as I see fit.
So I tidy up - easy and quick - if more is needed
   put off and, piled, a mess here and there.
   no time to care.
Much more exciting to pick up a book on my stack -
   read randomly - a delight to fill the creativity well, feels oh so good.
Image, word, line or quote - treasured and noted for future use.

Part of day's spent in front of a screen
   emails, online courses, a challenge to keep up
   And there too, I find so much to fill my creativity cup.
And every now and then, to the drawing board I go
   my being moves to doing. creating with the flow.
   Time stands still, a moment of ecstasy

With meals and other distractions
Day ends with satisfaction.

Grateful for the opportunity, I am who I am. Daring to be me.

Spring Dance

The beat and rhythm has changed
Winter's slow, plodding hum rearranged
An early morning trill of birds announce
Time to get moving and jump, with a bounce.

Just as my body gets into gear
Reminding me that, yes, Spring is here
We take a step back and it's winter again
but just for a moment as snow turns to rain.

Time for beginnings, a lush time of year
Frozen creek, cracking, flowing with cheer
Spirit bursting, budding, new dreams to explore
Like crocus and jonquils dancing once more.

Springtime Magic

Persephone yawns, stirs, stretches and sighs
  - the long time of underland sleep ending -
Struggling, wanting not to leave the darkened dreamtime
    or the reflective meanderings and wanderings of soultime

Slowly emerging from winter's cave of mystery
Breathing in fresh air
Feeling the warming sun kissing skin - relishing its tender touch
Shining worm moon sharing secrets of growing, sensing magic
Cooling rain, quenching a deep thirst,
nourishing early buds and sprouts
Opening eyes of the heart filled with desire and longing.

Feeling a gentle nudge, moving into discovery
Soaring spirits fly an eagle's dance of light
Gazing Nature's miracle of life
    soft gentle green canopy clothing dark, bare limbs,
    a flowering, colorful carpet spreading its brilliance .

Gathering her basket filled with urgings
Turning Wheel of Life - new cycle, new beginning.
No time to waste - each moment precious
With grateful heart - embrace wonder and delight.

Morning Silence

Slipping outside into the silence
Receiving the gift of no sound
A brief moment suspended in the void
Until awareness tunes in to my world around.

My breath so many times unnoticed
   stirs the air gently like butterfly wings
   softly until a deep exhale extended
   whooshes into the quiet, gratitude it brings.

Brother Wind, I hear your presence
   through the stately pines
   through the needled strings
A heavenly song reveals your essence.

Blessings of the moment abruptly ended
Sound bites of a new morn fill the air
Birds' melodies merrily greet the day
How does it get better than this, I say.

Spring

Sap, slowly seeping upwards toward outstretched arms
awakening slumbering giants of the earth, sounding the spring alarm.

Pared branches, bared and cold patiently await
a new soft-green leafy coat to emanate.

Raucous black bird perched on borrowed branch calls its song
inviting others to harmonize and sing along.

Inside, the tree soul quivering, quickening with delight
the turn of the year wheel, marked by a new ring, its rite.

Nest building, a yearly chore begun, a scavenger hunt for finding
the treasured twig, a bit of fur; persistent search demanding.

Gratitude for this time of year, a new beginning to discover
copious profound lessons, from Teacher Tree to uncover.

Love Notes

This is me wondering about the wanderings of my mind
the shoulda-woulda-coulda - s leaving me behind.

This is a new day, grateful for my Present
choices to be made, make each moment count.

This is me feeling cool of morn wanting warmth of sun
listening to the hum of cars blending with birds' morning songs

This is my home in pine-forested foothills where my soul belongs
mid rocky ground and mountain peaks all around.

This is me admiring nature through plate-glass windows
breathing in contentment, gazing at the beauty, sitting at the table.

This is my life with many years behind me, with far less ahead
sharing with family and friends, laughing with glee,
and breaking bread.

This is me doing the best I can, releasing what no longer serves me
filling my days with intentioned joy, creating and evolving
who I am.

A Celebration

The sound of snow
   Like sound of one hand clapping
Dwells inside, sweet winter's song
   to cool and soothe the heat of sun.

A song of wind gentle or pushing
   my dance; my life it's guiding
to bend and sway with whatever comes along
   or stilled in silence, bless-ed resting.

A bud thrusting through the ground
   Another year has come around
A birth-ing celebration, spring-ness
Infusing energy - keep growing - life is good.

Rising Spring

Stumbling through the mirrored hallways of my mind
Fractal images of who I am or I could be
Pieced together, a crazy-quilted pattern, a one-ness to explore
Found reflected in barren chamber, in sole/soul I see

For there I stand - memories flooding - life's well
   each storied droplet adding to the depth -
      all the years I've left behind
Tears of sorrow, tears of joy; I add with each new breath

And there in dappled ripples new fragments do appear
   Through eyes of the heart each watery ring
   a knowing it will bring
Follow the beckoning of the quiet voice inside
Do what you love, follow your dream, the Spring is rising.

Spring Haiku

Yesterday sunny
Today snow on the ground
Spring in the Rockies

Holy Fool

One who comes as Holy Fool
Stands beside me, lives inside me
Mother, Mentor, Mirror, Muse
    there to guide me or a ruse
    to find balance, wisdom, or amuse?
Her medicine is very strong
    at times thinking it's no good, trust me, she says, it's never wrong.

The beat of the earth lives within her
    pulsing steadily, drumming softly
the pace is kept, strumming along
      a chaotic cadence stirs things up.
    Get moving she says, stagnation's not allowed
      see the waters flowing, washing out the clouds.
    Dive deep, for in the dark, a pearl can be found

Sweet trickster teacher ever so fair
Messages profound you gently share
    with eyes of the heart, meaning will appear
    the price to pay at times is very dear.
        Steady as the old oak stands
        Always there to lend a hand
           My Happy Fool.

Spring Snow

Sitting at the table, gazing out the window
Snow resting on deck's rail, covering pine branches
   a white comforter all around.
The world is slowly waking, though the sun
   no hurry in breaking, a grey cloudy day
   greets me on this spring morn.

Snow, like a sound-deprivation chamber
   no sound, muffled sounds, the sound of embrace.
How can the cold feel so warm?
Feeling cocooned, protected, filled with grace.
   wondering what the day will bring, To-Do's not with-standing,
Ruminating, dreaming on the menu please.

At the front door standing, cold seeping into bone,
   looking at the whitened garden bed, new spring flowers peaking
   hoping soon the warm will reappear.
A sole tulip cut yesterday, brought inside -
   slowly opening with the warmth - Spring's budding delight.
Mother Nature's nudge to wake up and see the light.

Slow Moving to Nature's Song

Slow stepping with deep easy breathing
Deep listening to wind's sweet song
Slow dancing to earth's soothing rhythm
Swaying with the pine trees, moving oh so strong.

Stretching out with wild embrace
Inhaling deeply Nature's healing air
Scented with wonder and delight
It's everyone's gift if we only care.

Slow stepping with deep easy breathing …

Jumping with exuberance wildly
Sun ignites creative sparks
Spirit filled from beauty bathing
Slow down, she murmurs, I'm not going anywhere.

Slow stepping with deep easy breathing …

Bowing low in veneration
Her gifts to receive and employ.
She waits patiently for her revelation
to inform us and enjoy.

Slow stepping with deep easy breathing …

Spring Snow -
Call and Response
with Margaret Wildflower

Weather Goddess playing games
It's springtime in the Rockies after all.
Will she don her Spring dress and dancing shoes
Not today she says as snow starts to fall.

Plans change, get rearranged
No outing nor driving down the mountain,
There's ice beneath the cover, too risky to discover.
Stay inside, slipping and sliding not allowed.

Texting messages, sharing with delight
Knowing Spellcheck will right the wrongs playfully.
Discovering there's a poem, riffing poetically
Spontaneous magic, clarity comes easily

Meditate on wisdom of the snowflake
Listen to the snowflakes, sound of silence,
Close your eyes so you can see
See with your ears and listen with your eyes
Best when seen with eyes of the heart.
When the heart knows the mind is listening, love is born

Find two identical snowflakes to pass the time.
Certainly better than a snowy ride,

An old Native American saying shared
"Never ride your horse if it's not fun."
A chuckle rose not at this great wisdom
    but because of this great wisdom
    often ignored and/or not heard.
Have fun and listen to the snowflake - no ride today.

Ode to a New Pen

Simple joys - writing with a new pen
  with flowing ink inside, like blood coursing through my veins
  without the blessed fluid, nothingness resides.

Memories of fountain pens whose desiccated bodies
  I store lovingly, clinging to pleasures past
  I now rejoice with a new friend hoping the use will last.

Penmanship, calligraphy different nibs required
  and now perhaps for sketching, a new skill to try
  I eagerly begin - don't let the pen run dry.

Pleasures lost, pleasures regained, choices to be made.
  Easier to use the pens of current day - gel tips, felt tips,
  and many other kinds, when ink runs out discard and buy a new.

With fountain pen when ink runs out, do not throw out
  fill the well and continue on with fresh energy.
  I find myself filled with creative possibility.

A Light Goes Out

Sad news received today - with disbelief and dismay.
How, why and other questions surface trying to make sense
   of the inevitable reality coming unexpected
   - a life's journey coming to an end.

For sixteen years, like minded souls have met
   with common purpose for art and the creative process to discuss
   with books covering the gamut of topics, inspiring our lives.

Unique, disparate individuals sharing and caring.
Stories told on pages bound, stories of our lives
   hardly ever told - secrets about ourselves held like a vise.

Laughter, tears, not always to agree, for points of view
   we each hold dear - it's the connection and conviction that
   we each make a difference that is the glue.

We gather at the altar of our books, circling to feed our souls.
We are candles glowing with fiery spirit, the first
   snuffed out to be relit when next we meet beyond.

Farewell, Dear Fellow-Textie, we bid you sweet adieu
your voice will still be heard, your spirit felt
until once again, in the restaurant in the sky we'll gather
   reading books about our favorite things.

Until then, we'll raise our glass with laughter and tears
for new memories to make while deciding whose turn next
to pick the book - hope it's one that's easy and short
to inspire us as we keep moving on.

Until we meet again, we celebrate your passionate, creative life!

Doing Lunch

I must be getting older - time is flying past …
   the days go by so fast …
And I can't remember when I saw you last.

So happy we connected, emails and phone calls made
   to get together, as long as it's good weather.
Plans arranged - day, time and place to meet.
A new place to try where we can eat
   where the food is tasty, ambience low-key, not loud
   and not to feel rushed,
   as eating and catching up calmly is what it's all about.

Smiles and hugs the ritual begins
Sitting at the table conversation commences
   between menu perusing, checking the specials of the day
   hard to decide as we have so much to say.
Soon food arrives and a familiar rhythm appears
eating, talking, sharing what's happening in our lives
   since the last time we met.

Reminiscing about moments shared,
Life's hardships and challenges acknowledged
Concerns about world affairs abound
wondering if wisdom will ever be found
hoping for change that will truly make a difference
Praying that it happens in our lifetime is our preference.

Then much too soon our time disappears
promises made to do it again soon - repeated like a song
Smiles and hugs again - now with bellies full - the ritual ends
It's more than feeding the body - it's been food for the soul.

Taking measure - Glass Full

It's taken me a lifetime to get where I am today.
Seven decades then some - still learning every day, discovering
what I have to say.
Some questions new, some very old, as I ponder what life this is.
So many stories to be told, I'll bend your ear for sure, if I may.

Defining moments, now that's quite the list
Still adding story-bead adventures - hard to resist -
   to life's necklace recording secrets, events, people and places
   some threaded with tears, others with laughter and grace.

I ponder about my legacy - aging well begins my litany.
My epitaph perhaps, "A life well lived, well loved."
I make my destiny.
To pull this off, engaging the Creative Spirit, on this I depend
   to inform and inspire, to help me smile until the very end.

Memorial Day

A celebratory weekend in town
   and quiet is all around; hearing not a sound
to greet the day, on this mountain morn
no stirring yet, it's early still
   and with the stillness comes a reckoning.

Hustle and bustle is the order of the day
   Boulder Creek Festival, SugarLoaf Garage Sale,
Bolder/Boulder Marathon all add to the tale
   of merry making and … maybe for a moment
   pausing to think what there is to celebrate.

To commemorate the illustrious lives
   of those lost in war in a time of combat and strife.
Remember, commemorate, memorial - rooted in memory
   a word bringing up stories held inside - and
   a moment of silence, a prayer for our shared history.

Everyday Blessings

We don't realize how wonderful today is until tomorrow.
- Amish Proverb

Tomorrow is too late to see the preciousness of this moment
So what is it I can do to celebrate with contentment
   in this moment of sorrow or pain, hard to see what there is to gain.
Breathe in, Inhale strength. Trust in the Universe again and again.

Yesterday, late afternoon thundershowers blew in
Dark skies, sun hiding, drum rolls thundering in the clouds
Deep slow rumblings, sonorous lumbering all around
like heavy furniture scraping across heavenly ground

Today, too weary, confused, sad and amused
   pushing to move through the present with a smile
Knowing current soul discomfort will soon pass
Living in gratitude makes it all worthwhile.

Yesterday, I cherished the storm mimicking my inner chaos
Heavenly Cacophonous Concerto penetrating every cell
Jet engine roared in sync with its accented reverberation
Sharp, loud thunderous clap, crack of lightning and illumination.

Tomorrow, a clear calm day will arrive
Melancholic cobwebs washed away for the soul to survive
Not meant to live in the doom and the gloom
Count blessings, do what you love - like rain feeding the bloom.

Thank you for the Present.

Summer

Summer Solstice

Summer memories ...
Snow-cones, swinging, shorts, Sun fun
bring smiles forever.

Summer time living
How does it get better than this?
Fresh fruits and veggies

Summer time dreaming
Floating on river of life.
Open to what's next.

In Company of Trees

I sit each morning with my friends
   a cup of coffee in my hand

I communicate without a sound
   knowing that they understand.

A new day begins, I breathe with a sigh,
   I take in the wisdom afar and nearby.

My story begins. I muse over bread,
   questions and possibilities dance in my head.

They listen, regardless of my meanderings
   to whatever point my ramblings bring.

The trees nod with a profound knowing,
   that bending with the wind allows steady growing.

Answers not easily proffered
   listening and accepting is what's gently offered.

I bid sweet adieu to your kind company
   awaiting tomorrow's lesson and wisdom so eagerly.

Streaming

Solar eclipse in the southern hemisphere,
   vibrations of its dark-day energy felt here.
Concurrent with July's New Moon in Cancer
   magnifies the eerie blackness sensed inside.

Messages received from beyond
   meanings deciphered and found
   to guide me through the hours today
   finding that often it's up to me to find the way.

What does it take to dive deep into the well?
Is that where my meaning and purpose will dwell?
Embrace life, feeling naïve in the doing
   open to clarity, self compassionate in the being.

Who am I? I ask each day…for surely
   I've changed, for the better, I pray.
What are my fears? What holds me back?
Searching for answers, think I'll cut me some slack.

Forest Forays

Breathe in the forest.
Breathe out the urbane and mundane.
A well-worn path marks the way
  walking without fear, I stop to pray.

Alone I am, but not for long
  for soon leaves twitter, what is that song?
A distant melody ricochets through the branches,
  nearby a response bursts out ever so strong.

Mushrooms break through rich, loamy earth,
  shelters for little ones scurrying about.
Here and there a wildflower so dear,
  graces the path with bright color, a moment of cheer.

A lost soul midst trees standing so tall,
  some bent by the wind, some stunted, some small.
Stories to tell, memories to share
  leafy ears open to heartfelt care.

Cocooned beneath a sun-filtered crown.
Admiring roots buried deep in the ground.
Its labyrinthine bark captures my gaze,
like life's map, its twists and turns amaze.

Lost in reverie, in deep meditation
Reflection of its life rings of history,
    marking milestones, yet time to move on
    back to the present with reverence and revelation.

                Not lost at all.

Ordinary Tuesday

Tuesday, the most ordinary day of the week
Passing the time ever so meek.
It's presence, in the line-up of days,
   spent in a haze, a blur, or a daze.

A gift has been given, notice the moment,
   a breath of fresh air, cool, crisp mountain air.
The wind sighs through the trees, waking the pines
   and the bright yellow irises smile ever so fair.

Doing the laundry, mundane, mindless task
   washer and dryer make it easier and fast.
Happiness is fresh, clean-smelling clothes
   makes me feel good all the way to my toes.

Reframe the ordinary and plain
   like water into wine.
Magic happens, the enchantment begins
   soon dazzle gets under my skin.

The ordinary was extraordinary today.

The Measure of One's Worth

Wherein does the creative spirit lie?
In the small hands of a five year old making a mud pie
    deftly transformed into a figure with the clay she plied,
    in spite of whipping endured for the "graven image" of her creation,
    leaving a remarkable legacy of her spirit-full expression.

She became a committed sculptor with limited acclaim
    in her lifetime; now gone she basks in the fame
    today I learn of your birth February 29, 1892 and your name,
    Augusta Savage, news of your retrospective on the radio came.
In the pages of art history, a place you now rightfully claim.

You lived your "one wild and precious life"
    as only you knew how, following the voice within;
Head held high, ever present with beauty evolving
    your meaning and purpose we learn of now,
    your talent and wisdom with students you shared.

Color of skin, gender, circumstances, and challenging attacks
    did not hold your creative conviction and determination back.
Her-story exposed, celebrated and profound
    for us to find courage and inspiration in her present-day renown.
Does it always take hindsight to grasp the full measure of a life?

Remember When

What were you doing fifty years ago?
Like a bucket of cold water poured over me
a flood of memories washed me fresh
startling my senses, awakening sleeping giants.

Degree in hand, struggling to find a career
my future trajectory was not very clear.
Events of the world, challenging at best
    for the race to the moon gave our country no rest.

An unknown, uncertain undertaking, too risky to plan
but the certain goal we must make. - Put a man on the moon.
Scientific community, aflutter, jumping hurdles
    for winning the race is what it's about, and it had to be soon.

To be first, the competition very intensive
fueling creative fires, leading the offensive.
A feat so improbable, impossible for some
    methodically, magically the launch, the walk did come.

The first man on the moon, fifty years ago history was made
as millions watched grainy images on the TV, compelling reality.
With awe, wonder, disbelief - tears of joy dispelled the fear
    for mission accomplished, a memory now held dear.

A salute to Neil Armstrong, first man on the moon
   first words, a momentous utterance,
"A small step for man, a giant leap for mankind."
Follow your dream, it's meant to encourage and remind,
Remembering it takes many for solutions to discover

Hats off to all who made Apollo 11 Mission a stunner.

Summer Sizzle

Summer sun cresting on the horizon
   Early morning rays set the tone of the day
   Three digit temperatures to crawl across the land
     scorching and searing; a reckoning at hand?

What is it that I like to do on a hot summer day?
   Time for wool gathering, remembering hot summers past
     watermelon, peaches, strawberries, mangos to relish
     tomatoes and corn - all tasty gifts, memories I cherish.

Time to move slowly and mindfully - plan of the day
   keeping cool is my goal, nothing strenuous I say
   dreaming of what I'd like to do, floating on the river of life
   letting my pen run with it without much ado.

Words scramble together, made coherent,
   not rambling, is a task I like best
     Too hot for anything physical - as
     exertion would certainly demand rest.

Summertime - living easy, dreaming my time away
   thoughts of projects tumbling with only energy to play
Yet mindful of fleeting time, so precious like gold
     So I think I'll just read and dream of the cold.

Ode to a Hummingbird

Again I sit meditating on the beauty of nature
　　through plate-glass windows, my favorite perch.
Though I enjoy greeting the day from my front porch
　　it's inside looking out that soothes and inspires.

The view is spectacular, wooded foothills afar,
　　tall pine trees surround me, a wonder to behold.
Each day different mysteries revealed as I contemplate
　　and ask for clarity on how to proceed and be bold.

The response this morning so small and so fleeting
　　came up to my window, surely singing my name.
Watch closely it said, take in the light, all is in sight
　　and for a brief moment - stopped - showing me it's alright.

Oh, hummingbird you bring me great joy,
　　reminding me that the journey is part of the plan.
The coming and going, facing the doing as best as we can,
　　and being in the moment is the wisdom at hand.

September Moon

Night noises change their cadence
  in the beginning of the day
  the soft, sonorous sighing
  shifting to a new song.

Dream waves coming to an end
Snippets of night mystery stories
  ... held on to
  its meaning to understand.

Harvest Moon rising in Pisces
  its beacon shone brightly
    announcing the morn.
Awareness of light awakening,
  my sleepy head - pillowed in rest.

Too early to greet the day
    return to bed
futile attempts to slumber again ...
  I ruminate, I meditate and
    get up instead.

Humbled by the moon's power and magic
  its cyclical rhythms move
  waters, mark the season.
Embrace the light, absorb
  its wisdom ... listen
  Listen to its reason.

Out of the Wild

time spent in cages, to save them
   the raptors
   to heal the wounds inflicted
   mostly human carelessness, negligence

what happens to the wild
   price to pay for surviving
   trained to return, flying free

human care, human love …then
   retrained … choice to embrace the wild again

yet so many choose to remain, to return.

Peaches and Dreams

I tasted Canadian sun
   slivers of dried peaches for breakfast
   infused with love of land
   from labored hands of a friend.

Many years she moved away
   searching for a better life
   leaving unpleasant political strife
   discovering a passion to follow.

An orchard, an owner old and tired
   sold his legacy of what he held dear.
Challenge embraced, do it right,
   green ways, organic she set her sight.

Here I sit so far away
   succulent juices fill my veins
Memories of picking peaches
   smiles of sweetness remain.

Autumn

Stepping Into Life

Engaging. Moving. Stepping.
   Discovering the world around
   testing the ground testing the waters
               small steps.

Tentative, unbalanced, finding equilibrium,
   stumbling, stepping, falling -
               getting up
      Falling - getting up
      falling - getting up
      again and again
               till mastery found.

Footfall on hallowed ground
   impressions made deep
Marking place in the world.
Repeating the ritual
   gaining presence
   steadier and steadier
   with firmness asserting essence.

With oldness comes boldness
   measured steps, slowness
   awareness of footprints
      made on fragile earth.

Conundrum to ponder
    leave no trace
Spirit walking
    ghosts of place
Sense of who I am
    a mere wisp of grace.

Autumn

A we-filled souls for millennia attuned to nature's cycles
Admired, enjoyed, relished the harvest

U niversal truth, reaping the sown
Embedded in our bones,
A pause to embody the wisdom of the earth

T antalizing scents of ripened bounty
of rich, loamy earth
Memories of simple, sumptuous feasts swell the heart

*U*sing eyes and ears of the heart
Profound mystery of season understood
Senses alerted to all that's good.

M other Nature with flowing, natural rhythm, soothing,
Easing one to let go. Cast away what's no longer serving.

*N*ature provides its cyclic wisdom of pausing to give thanks
for the richness of abundance deserves a merry dance.

The Light Within

Do not be afraid
   Have no fear
It's your darkness held so dear.

There is a light within
   It's wonder awaiting, waiting.

The dark night of the soul
   begging for awakening
Stirrings of unrest, dis-ease
   longing for clarity
Illumination, please.

There is dawn
   returning faithfully
Eos, Aurora, Sol
   emerging peacefully.

Remove the darkened glance
   time to face the day.

Wonder brightens the flame
   The Present is a - glow

Breathe in the light
   Embrace with enlightened eyes.

Train to Nowhere

Where is the mind
  when the brain no longer remembers?
Forgotten words, unfamiliar familiar faces, strange places,
  memories lost behind doors in a haunted house.
What remains?

In the mind's eye, a scrambled scene painful to unscramble?
What does it see in this new landscape
  of never-ending sea?
My loving eyes gazing at that soulful, confused look
  both longing for small glimpses of what life used to be.

This journey is the hardest.
The train bound to Nowhere.
Destination unknown and then
  from the darkened tunnel, a ray of light beaming
  as a smile, made it all worthwhile

        for Love remembers.

As Darkness Grows

Darkness slowly slithering
   pushing back the sunrise
   hastening the sunset
The wheel of the year
   turned tilting my axis
   daily rhythms changing.

Changes mark the season
   what is happening now?
Nature's slowing down
   blooms, fallen leaves
   decaying on the ground
   preparing for what's coming next.

Busy scurrying, a time
   for wrapping up
   year's end not far away
So what is it that I do today?
Endings frenzied pending with noted action
Beginnings surging, quiet mindfulness, dark-time reflection.

Cocooning in the dark
Reveling in the light
Beaver Moon, re-framing vision
Harvest Moon, soul-time tending
A time to reminisce, a time to subsist
most importantly, a time of grateful bliss.

ADVENT

Awe and wonder

Daily ritual

Vital vigilance

Eyes and ears of the heart

Nature's lessons

Time for reflection

Ritual for commemorating the waiting, the coming,
marked with fanciful or traditional calendar boxes
offering twenty-four, plus one, pocketfuls of treats
anticipating the trove of presents - a Christmas feast.

Wreath of green boughs, four candles encircled
lit weekly one-by-one increasing the light
dispelling the darkness of shortened days on earth
magical, mystical, symbol of an enlightened birth.

Season of the heart, peace and joy abound
Where does true meaning lie with Santa around?

Shifting Seasons

A conflicting time of year
The solar-year cycle coming to an end
The waning Autumn, soul bent on holding
   lingering memories of harvest bounty
   brilliant oranges, golds, reds and brown
   leaves dropped on ground and gone.

Trees skeletal in appearance, bared limbs
   clothed in whitened robes looking sublime
Weather announcers issuing winter weather advisories
   snow around while my heart, still attuned to Fall,
   claims that winter is days away after all.
For it's not the snow that marks the season.

Not snow but light registers the seasons' shift
Mysteries of the Universe, the Sun's delight
Shorter days, longer days
   a balance of dark and light
The passage of seasons: Winter, Spring, Summer, Fall
Soul garden's treasures enchant and enthrall

Endings

In Reflection

*Finish every day and be done with it. For manners and
for wise living it is a vice to remember. You have done
what you could; some blunders and absurdities no doubt
crept in; forget them as soon as you can. To-morrow is a
new day; you shall begin it well and serenely, and with too
high a spirit to be cumbered with your old nonsense.*
- Ralph Waldo Emerson

What am I feeling now as I come full circle? Beginnings-Endings.
Endings-Beginnings. I look back on what has transpired and I have
to shout out, "I did it!", and dance about. With a loud "Yahoo" and
many high-fives, I am filled with overflowing glee. Coming to the
end of a project may be inconsequential to many but I choose to
celebrate my accomplishment. How often do we deny ourselves
this reaction?

When I first stepped into the unknown territory of creating an
intentional poetic journal through four seasons, I had no clear
road map guiding my journey. Yes, I wanted to record my reaction
to and interaction with nature, people, places, and my feelings
through the power of poetry. This was a project which challenged
my usual way of being and doing. My inner critic at the start
admonished, "Sure you are excited and you'll do it for a while and
then before long you will stop and move on to something else."
That critical warning could be observed without much notice as
coming up with new ideas, new projects come easily. I count my
ideation and imagination as a strong suit. Completion on the other
hand is a challenge and struggle as I am master of "put off 'til

tomorrow". I set my compass on staying the course with help from family and friends. My bar for accomplishment was set at enjoying the process which became a self-fulfilling standard.

I fulfilled my intention to travel poetically through the seasons. Each day I gave nod to the wonder of the season. With daily reflection, I gained wisdom from tending to my soul's garden. I give pause to look back on what transpired, where I am today and what are my takeaways.

1) Showing up

I discovered the importance of space and place. Finding the special spot in our home where I could enter and be transported into my heart space was paramount in keeping me on track. It is my multi-purpose sanctuary for meditation, inspirational reading, creative writing, reflective writing, wool gathering, day dreaming and my poetic journaling. I learned that showing up early in the morning in that space before the busyness of the day took over, I could more easily engage my poetic muse.

2) Trusting the Process

I had no clear notion nor expectation of an outcome. My idea was to experience and savor the seasons and to record my observations. As I had joined a poetry group, I felt the push and desire to journal in poetic form rather than my typical narrative style. My goal was not to get up tight about my poetic style or caliber of writing and to have fun with word-play. Nor did I set a resolution for daily production. I chose to have the intention to do it as often as possible knowing that life at times gets in the way. A funny thing happened when I let go of judgment and expectations and just showed up. The more I did it, the more I would get ideas about what to write. From the fear of not knowing what I would write, I experienced the magic of being in the moment and allowing what would happen to happen.

3) Honoring the Journey

Little did I know that my sitting to write poems as a new form of journaling would result in the desire to collect my poems in book form. As the end of Autumn drew near, I sensed the inner unrest rising to celebrate my accomplishment in a manner which stood me on end, I listened to my soul's voice. Validation is a vital aspect of the creative process and I ended my journey by following my soul's urgings and deep longing to make my debut as a published writer. Of deeper value however, I noticed that it wasn't about what I did but rather the joy and pleasure I had on the journey. It was my engagement in the moment, in the process which inspired and guided my steps along the way.

4) What Next

It is so difficult not to feel a heaviness when a culmination of a project is met. The energy and momentum of the ongoing practice is still surging so continuing on is an option. I take a deep breath and wonder if this was a project with a start and finish or was I establishing a mindful and spiritual practice of deep observation, noticing, and recording my feelings, reactions, and reflections of the day. I know enhancements to my journaling practice may benefit from review. Perhaps a related or different creative project is an offshoot of what I have done this past year. I trust as this door closes, another opens. I am on the threshold of whatever it is I am meant to do. I listen to the voice within for

> Today I stand in wonder
> I walk in wisdom
> I am in spirit
> I am open to possibilities.

Journey's End

A poignant pause as the end draws near
   A year gone by, where do I go from here?
A time for reflection, what lessons learned?
   Take time to go deep, feeling the burn

Moving through seasons, a project intention
   discovering a life practice, paying attention.
A time commitment, sitting at the table
   words in poetry or prose whenever able

No regrets on days missed
   nature, walk-abouts, inspire and assist
Listening to soul's voices, name of the game
   with the Creative sure to engage

The moment now to turn the page
   a new venture or more of the same
Four seasons, a year, a decade now gone
   The past to release, time to move on

Tomorrow the start of a new day
   Trusting my spirit to guide the way
With open wonder embracing what's to come
   heart bursting in gratitude to greet the sun.

Acknowledgments

It is with deepest appreciation and gratitude that I hold dearly all upon whose shoulders I have stood and will continue to depend on to provide a creative, spiritual and moral compass to guide my journey.

To the magnificently creative women in the CreativeSage-ing Circle who have bravely journeyed with me producing a diverse and brilliant body of creative work and providing insights into the significance of living from wonder to wisdom and who continually inspire me to aim higher.

To the impassioned creatives of Text in the City Art Book Club who for 17years have inspired, challenged and delighted my journey with their book selections.

To the Positive Aging Group, under the leadership of H.R. Moody, author of ***The Five Stages of the Soul: Charting the Spiritual Passages That Shape Our Lives***, meeting over lunch and engaging in stimulating presentations and lively discussions on aspects of aging and living positively.

To the Sage-ing International Community and particularly its founder, Rabbi Zalman Schachter-Shalomi, author of ***From Age-ing to Sage-ing: A Revolutionary Approach to Growing Older*** who inform my personal spiritual and wisdom journey.

To Cat Caracelo, founder and Director of JourneyPath Institute whose vision and mission to provide transformative experiences through the modalities of expressive arts and visual narrative inspired me to become a JourneyCircles™ Licensed Facilitator and a certified Creative Depth Coach and to expand my personal creative vision. For information visit: https://journeypathinstitute.com/

To Jan Blencowe, visual artist, workshop facilitator, creative depth coach whose personal and professional journey inspires me through her insights into the creative process and her profound connection to nature and its relationship to creative expression. For information visit: https://janblencowe.com/

To the many creatives, artists, spiritual leaders, age-ing leaders, mentors and muses past and present whose lives have made a significant impact on who I am today: Lucien Wulsin, Rosemary Williams, Deborah Arnold, Lorraine Robinson, Elizabeth Nissley, Margaret Wildflower and my fellow members of the stone carving group, Banda Ancha: Beatriz Carbonell-Ferrer, Constantina Iconomopulos, and Brenda Oakes and to the others whose names are also carried in my heart. I cherish and honor your courage and wisdom.

To all with whom I have crossed paths especially the supportive and caring staff at Lulu Press: your spirit flows within and through me.

About the Author

Elsie Wood is a visual artist, writer, lecturer, coach and workshop facilitator. She is a seeker, life-long learner, creative, sage and visionary. Her eclectic mix of artistic, personal and professional background informs her creative vision.

She made a defining career change from the computer industry to the arts in her mid-thirties. Her passion for the creative process has provided the catalyst for personal growth and the development of her preferred artistic medium, sculpture, and the promotion of creativity in others.

Her artistic endeavors include art-making, exhibiting, participating in international sculpture symposia; and lecturing on, writing about, and teaching art. She has experience in organizational management in various capacities: founding several art organizations, strategic planning, facilitating meetings, conferences, and symposia. She was Executive Director for the Society for Creative Aging and Coordinator for Intergenerational Projects for the Children, Youth, and Environments Center, at the University of Colorado Environmental Design Department

She received her Master of Education in the field of Creative Arts in Learning from Lesley University in Cambridge, Massachusetts and is an alumna of Journey Path Institute as a JourneyCircles™ Licensed Facilitator and a certified Creative Depth Coach.

Engaging in the creative process as a way of being, living and doing, Elsie Wood has developed workshops, retreats, and courses to integrate Creativity, Age-ing and Sage-ing. She is currently facilitating a CreativeSage-ing Circle in Colorado. Her passion and vision is the impetus for founding the CreativeSage-ing Center. Her personal journey as a creative who is age-ing and sage-ing is the spark for her poetic imagination in this collection of poetry.

www.ingramcontent.com/pod-product-compliance
Lightning Source LLC
LaVergne TN
LVHW091204080426
835509LV00006B/826